This
Nature Journal
Belongs To:

_____

Nature Observation Tips:

- Use all of your senses and note the sights, smells and sounds all around you.

- Try going to the same place, about the same time, once every week to note the changes in the nearby environment.

- Look close to the ground. Check below the grass and under rocks. Look up into the trees. Especially on the branches, leaves and bark.

- Note the changing of the seasons. See the differences in the plants, insects and other animals.

- Look for animal signs and tracks left in the mud, or the places where creatures have chewed or burrowed.

- Go outside at night to listen to the sounds and watch for fireflies.

- Ask questions about the things you notice, and then do research to learn more!

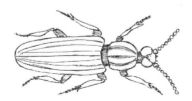

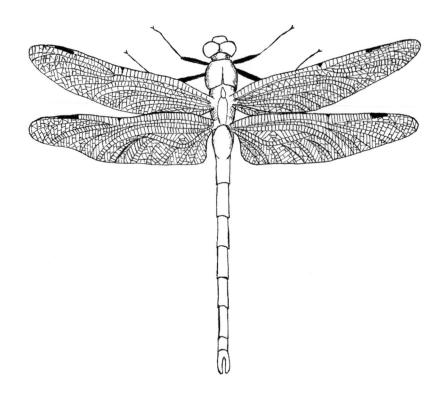

A Few Handy Supplies:

- Pencils and color pencils to record the things you see.

- Small jars or other containers for specimens.

- Magnifying glass or binoculars.

- Your favorite field guides.

- Your nature journal.

- A tote bag or backpack for your supplies.

- A snack or water (if you will be out long).

- A bandana or cloth handkerchief (for wiping hands, or picking up something you would rather not touch, or to carry home small items etc.)

- A hat or sunscreen.

- A healthy supply of curiosity and patience.

To Use This Journal:

- Simply sketch (or paste a photo of) your nature finds in the boxes provided on both sides of each entry spread. You can do this either while you are out in nature, or after you have returned home with your specimens.

- Record the date, location, time and weather, along with your observations and questions.

- Don't forget to draw a quick outline of the current moon phase and check either waxing or waning. If the moon is currently growing it is "waxing", if it is shrinking it is "waning".

- But more important than anything else, just *enjoy* being out in nature

Waxing Gibbous

Full Moon

Waning Gibbous

Phases *of the* Moon

Waxing Quarter

Waning Quarter

Waxing Crescent

Waning Crescent

New Moon

A Few Tracks

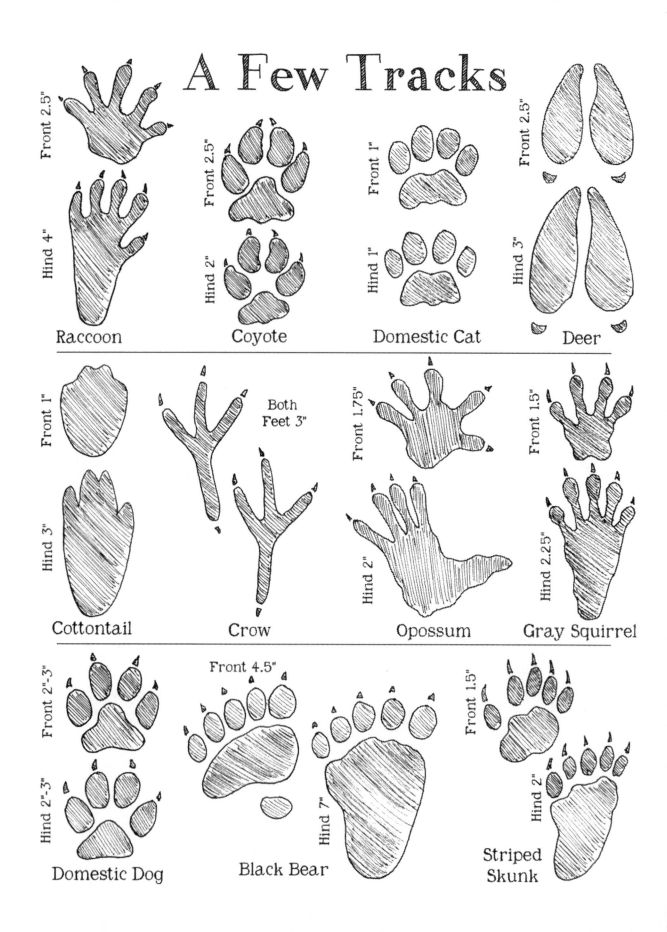

Front 2.5" Hind 4" Raccoon

Front 2.5" Hind 2" Coyote

Front 1" Hind 1" Domestic Cat

Front 2.5" Hind 3" Deer

Front 1" Hind 3" Cottontail

Both Feet 3" Crow

Front 1.75" Hind 2" Opossum

Front 1.5" Hind 2.25" Gray Squirrel

Front 2"-3" Hind 2"-3" Domestic Dog

Front 4.5" Hind 7" Black Bear

Front 1.5" Hind 2" Striped Skunk

Plants to Avoid!

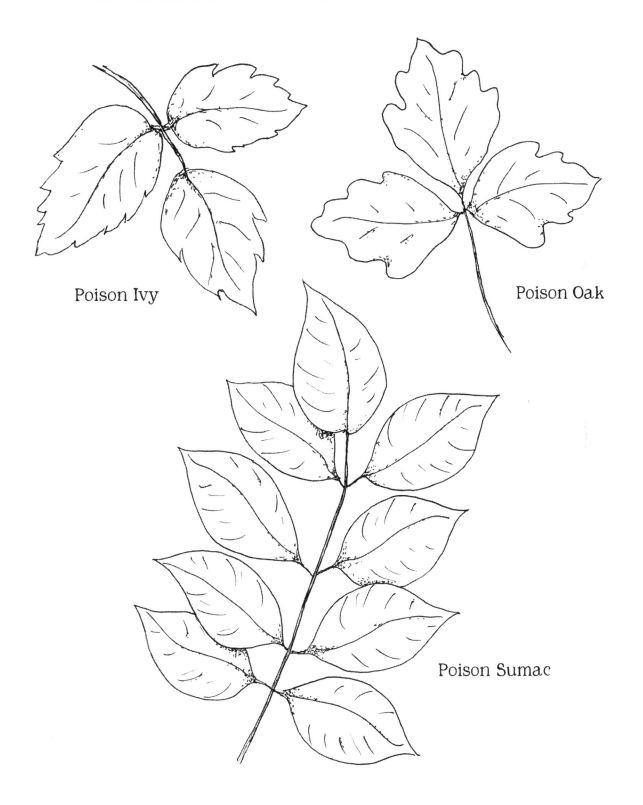

Poison Ivy

Poison Oak

Poison Sumac

"Look deep into nature,
and then you will
understand everything
better."

- *Albert Einstein*

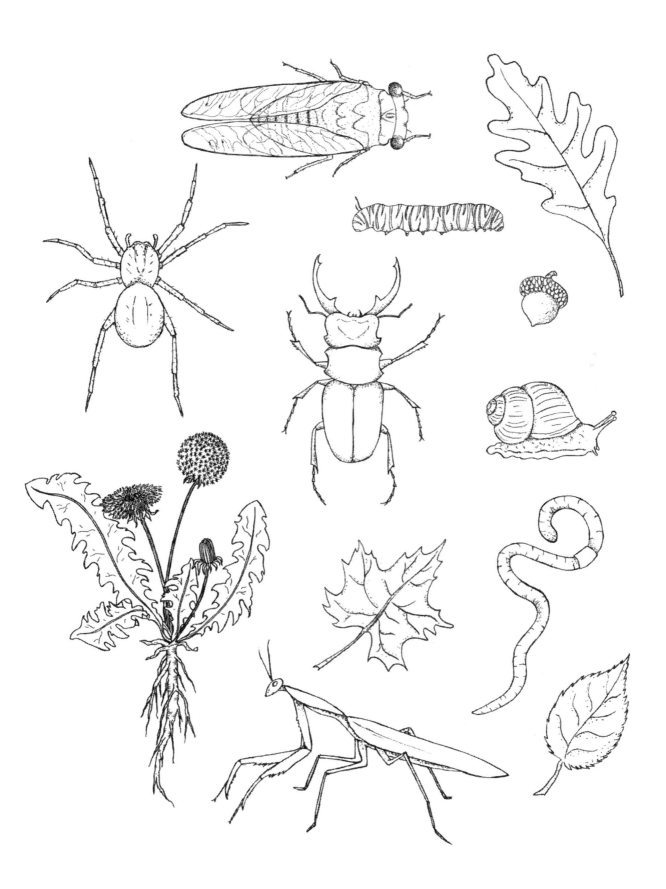

Date:

Lunar Phase

○ Waxing
○ Waning

Location:

Time: Weather:

Observations:

Questions:

More of What I Saw Today

Date:

Lunar Phase

O Waxing
O Waning

Location:

Time: Weather:

Observations:

Questions:

More of What I Saw Today

Date:

Lunar Phase

○ Waxing
○ Waning

Location:

Time: Weather:

Observations:

Questions:

More of What I Saw Today

Date:

Lunar Phase

O Waxing
O Waning

Location:

Time: Weather:

Observations:

Questions:

More of What I Saw Today

Date:

Lunar Phase

O Waxing
O Waning

Location:

Time: Weather:

Observations:

Questions:

More of What I Saw Today

Date:

Lunar Phase

O Waxing
O Waning

Location:

Time: Weather:

Observations:

Questions:

More of What I Saw Today

Date:

Lunar Phase

O Waxing
O Waning

Location:

Time: Weather:

Observations:

Questions:

More of What I Saw Today

Date:

Lunar Phase

O Waxing
O Waning

Location:

Time: Weather:

Observations:

Questions:

More of What I Saw Today

Date:

Lunar Phase

O Waxing
O Waning

Location:

Time: Weather:

Observations:

Questions:

More of What I Saw Today

Date:

Lunar Phase

○ Waxing
○ Waning

Location:

Time: Weather:

Observations:

Questions:

More of What I Saw Today

Date:

Lunar Phase

○ Waxing
○ Waning

Location:

Time: Weather:

Observations:

Questions:

Date:

Lunar Phase

○ Waxing
○ Waning

Location:

Time: Weather:

Observations:

Questions:

More of What I Saw Today

Date:

Lunar Phase

O Waxing
O Waning

Location:

Time: Weather:

Observations:

Questions:

More of What I Saw Today

Date:

Lunar Phase

O   Waxing
O   Waning

Location:

Time: Weather:

Observations:

Questions:

More of What I Saw Today

Date:

Lunar Phase

○ Waxing
○ Waning

Location:

Time: Weather:

Observations:

Questions:

More of What I Saw Today

Date:

Lunar Phase

○ Waxing
○ Waning

Location:

Time: Weather:

Observations:

Questions:

More of What I Saw Today

Date:

Lunar Phase

O   Waxing
O   Waning

Location:

Time: Weather:

Observations:

Questions:

More of What I Saw Today

Date:

Lunar Phase

O Waxing
O Waning

Location:

Time: Weather:

Observations:

Questions:

More of What I Saw Today

Date:

Lunar Phase

○ Waxing
○ Waning

Location:

Time: Weather:

Observations:

Questions:

More of What I Saw Today

Date:

Lunar Phase

O Waxing
O Waning

Location:

Time: Weather:

Observations:

Questions:

More of What I Saw Today

Date:

Lunar Phase

O Waxing
O Waning

Location:

Time: Weather:

Observations:

Questions:

More of What I Saw Today

Date:

Lunar Phase

○ Waxing
○ Waning

Location:

Time: Weather:

Observations:

Questions:

Date:

Lunar Phase

○ Waxing
○ Waning

Location:

Time: Weather:

Observations:

Questions:

More of What I Saw Today

Date:

Lunar Phase

○ Waxing
○ Waning

Location:

Time: Weather:

Observations:

Questions:

More of What I Saw Today

Date:

Lunar Phase

○ Waxing
○ Waning

Location:

Time: Weather:

Observations:

Questions:

More of What I Saw Today

Date:

Lunar Phase

○ Waxing
○ Waning

Location:

Time: Weather:

Observations:

Questions:

More of What I Saw Today

Date:

Lunar Phase

○ Waxing
○ Waning

Location:

Time: Weather:

Observations:

Questions:

More of What I Saw Today

Date:

Lunar Phase

O Waxing
O Waning

Location:

Time: Weather:

Observations:

Questions:

Date:

Lunar Phase

○ Waxing
○ Waning

Location:

Time: Weather:

Observations:

Questions:

More of What I Saw Today

Date:

Lunar Phase

○ Waxing
○ Waning

Location:

Time: Weather:

Observations:

Questions:

More of What I Saw Today

Date:

Lunar Phase

○ Waxing
○ Waning

Location:

Time: Weather:

Observations:

Questions:

More of What I Saw Today

Date:

Lunar Phase

○ Waxing
○ Waning

Location:

Time: Weather:

Observations:

Questions:

Date:

Lunar Phase

○ Waxing
○ Waning

Location:

Time: Weather:

Observations:

Questions:

More of What I Saw Today

Date:

Lunar Phase

○ Waxing
○ Waning

Location:

Time: Weather:

Observations:

Questions:

More of What I Saw Today

Date:

Lunar Phase

○ Waxing
○ Waning

Location:

Time: Weather:

Observations:

Questions:

More of What I Saw Today

Date:

Lunar Phase

O Waxing
O Waning

Location:

Time: Weather:

Observations:

Questions:

More of What I Saw Today

Date:

Lunar Phase

O Waxing
O Waning

Location:

Time: Weather:

Observations:

Questions:

More of What I Saw Today

Date:

Lunar Phase

O Waxing
O Waning

Location:

Time: Weather:

Observations:

Questions:

Date:

Lunar Phase

○ Waxing
○ Waning

Location:

Time: Weather:

Observations:

Questions:

More of What I Saw Today

Date:

Lunar Phase

○ Waxing
○ Waning

Location:

Time: Weather:

Observations:

Questions:

More of What I Saw Today

Date:

Lunar Phase

○ Waxing
○ Waning

Location:

Time: Weather:

Observations:

Questions:

More of What I Saw Today

Date:

Lunar Phase

○ Waxing
○ Waning

Location:

Time: Weather:

Observations:

Questions:

More of What I Saw Today

Date:

Lunar Phase

○ Waxing
○ Waning

Location:

Time: Weather:

Observations:

Questions:

More of What I Saw Today

Date:

Lunar Phase

○ Waxing
○ Waning

Location:

Time: Weather:

Observations:

Questions:

More of What I Saw Today

Date:

Lunar Phase

O Waxing
O Waning

Location:

Time: Weather:

Observations:

Questions:

More of What I Saw Today

"In every walk with
nature one receives far
more than he seeks.

- *John Muir*

Made in the USA
Middletown, DE
01 June 2021